A Mark Dahle Portfolio

Roger's Well

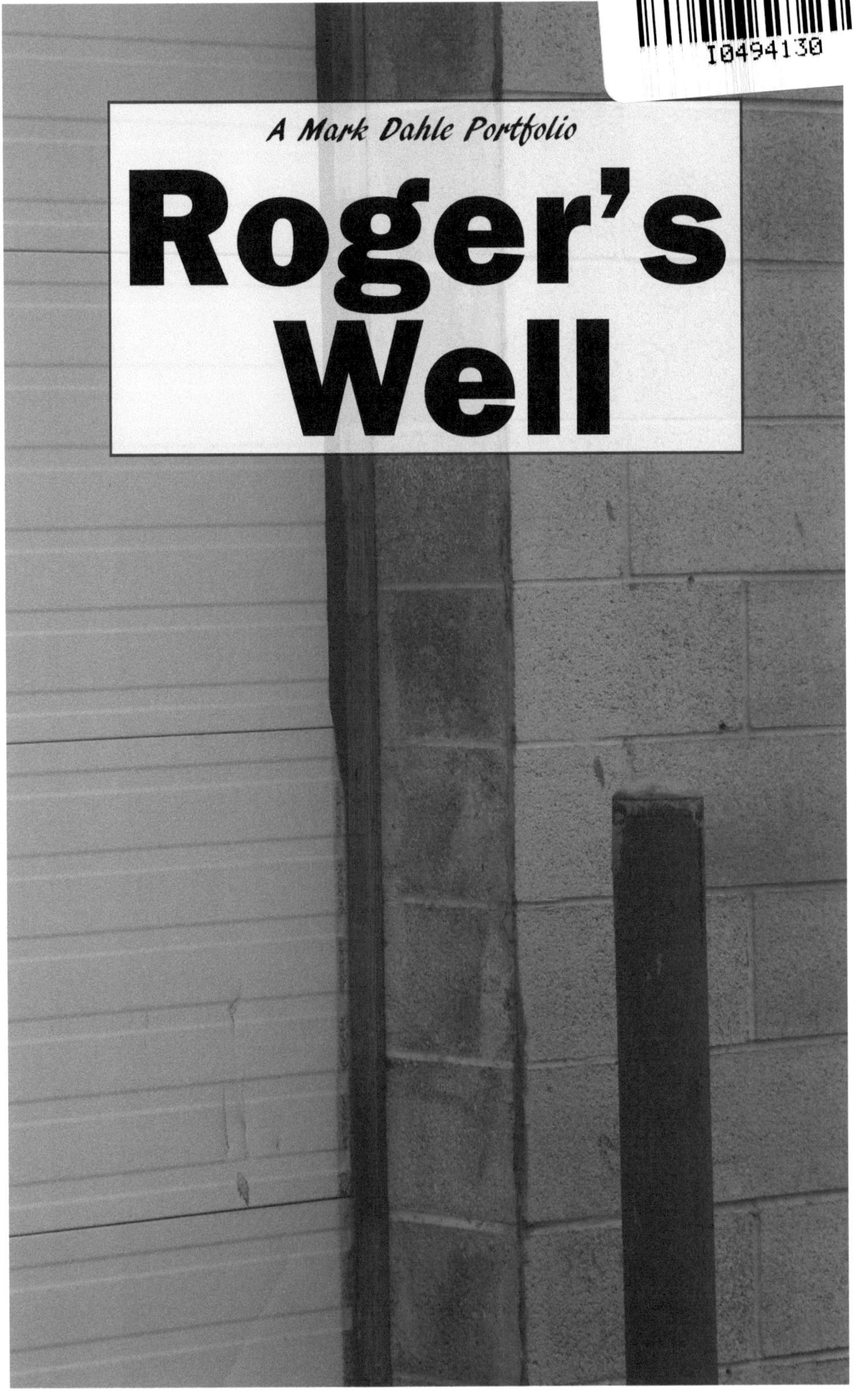

Mark Dahle Portfolios can be read in a few minutes and enjoyed for a lifetime.

This portfolio includes a story about an exhausted man digging a well, a photo of a beautiful 24 x 36 inch painting (at the right) and twenty-six outstanding photographs, mostly from Minneapolis.

Unlike many picture books, the text is unrelated to the painting and photographs. This might seem a little weird at first. One thing that makes it better is to order more portfolios until you get used to it. In the meantime, space is provided on the pages for you to draw your own pictures of wells if you like.

Photographs in this book are available in limited editions. See http://www.MarkDahle.com for more information and for previews of upcoming portfolios.

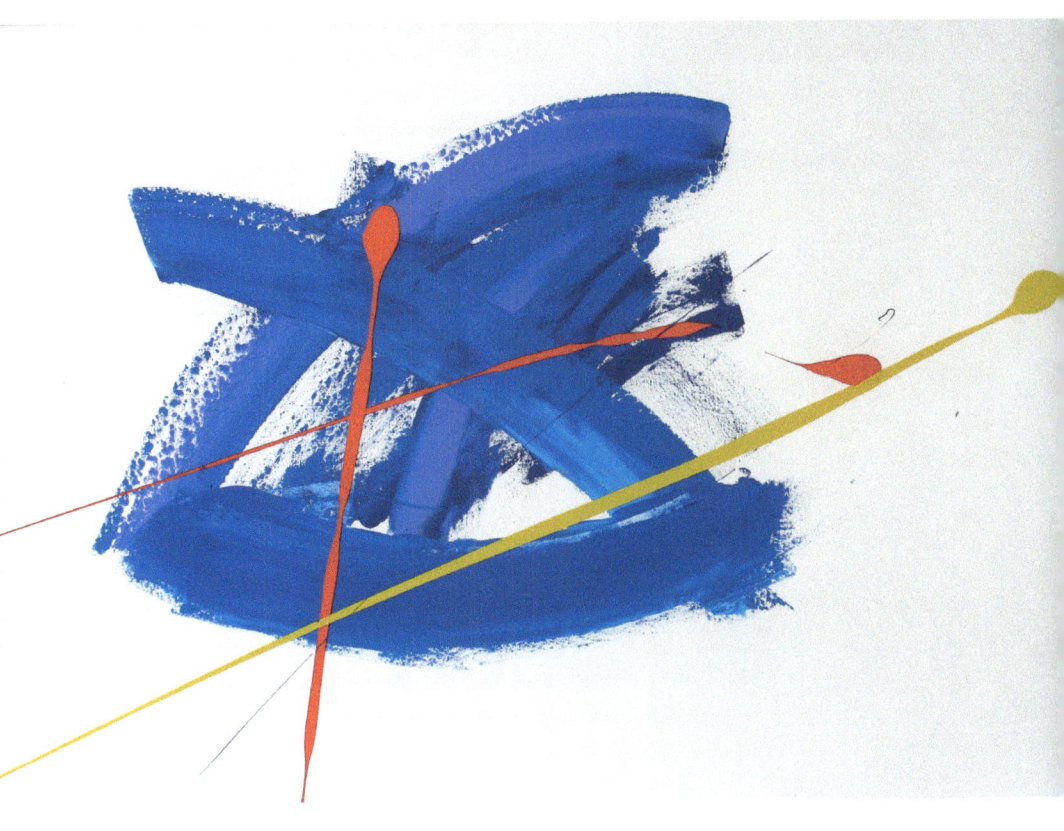

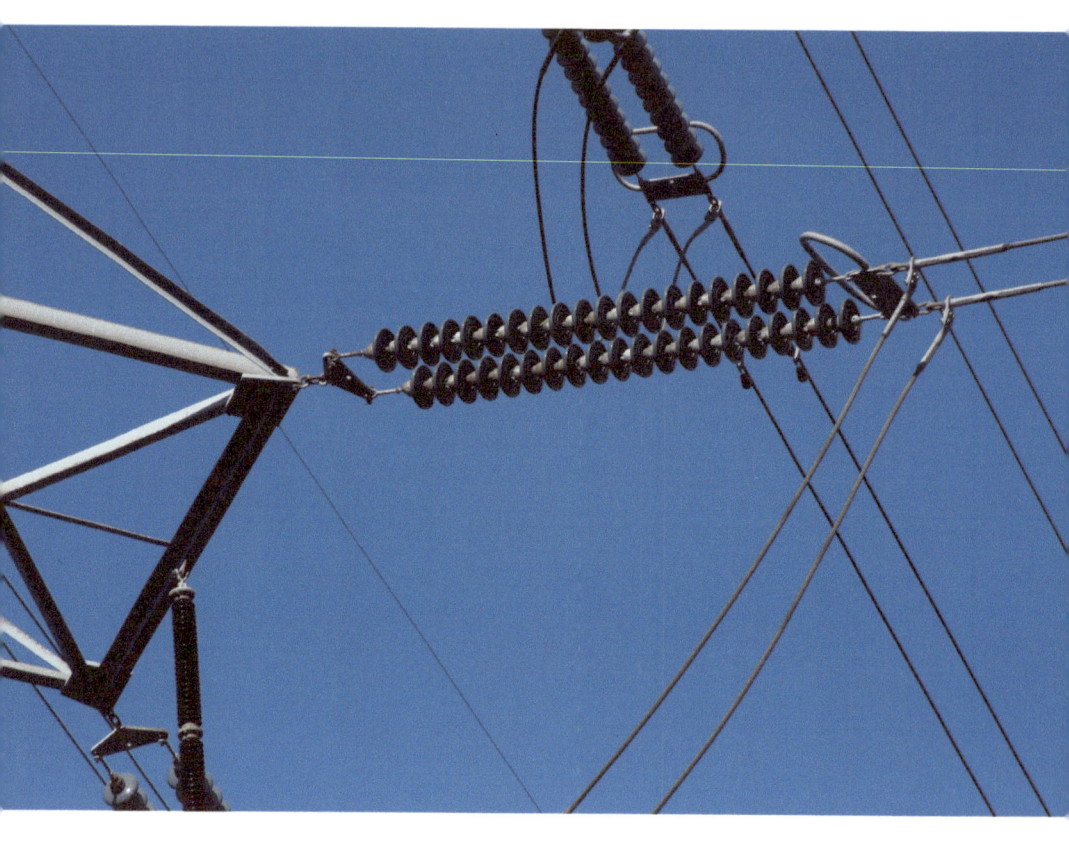

~ ~ ~

I'm going to tell you something
Roger didn't know.

The water was at a depth of 61 feet.

Roger *thought* there might be water.
He *hoped* there was water.
But he wasn't sure.

All he knew was that he *needed* water,
and he was going to dig a well
to try to get some.

In the morning
Roger dug down six feet.
His digging produced nothing.

He dug another six feet that afternoon.

Hard work.
Sweat.
Sore muscles.
But no water.

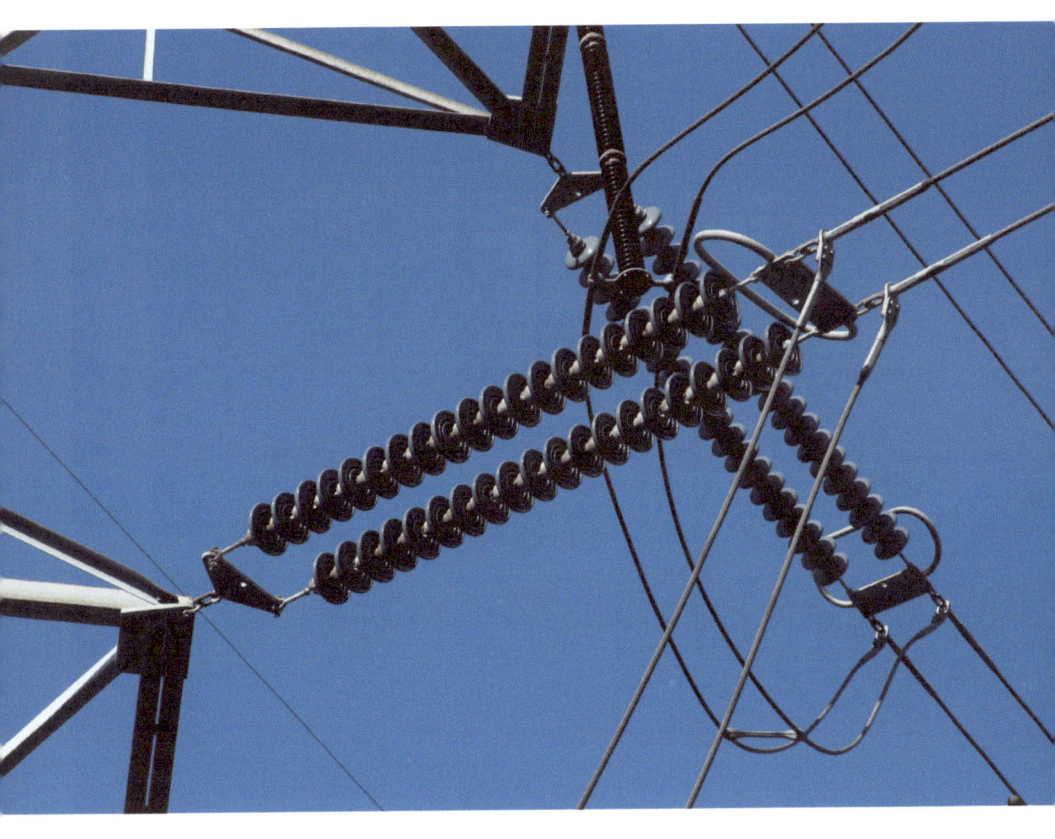

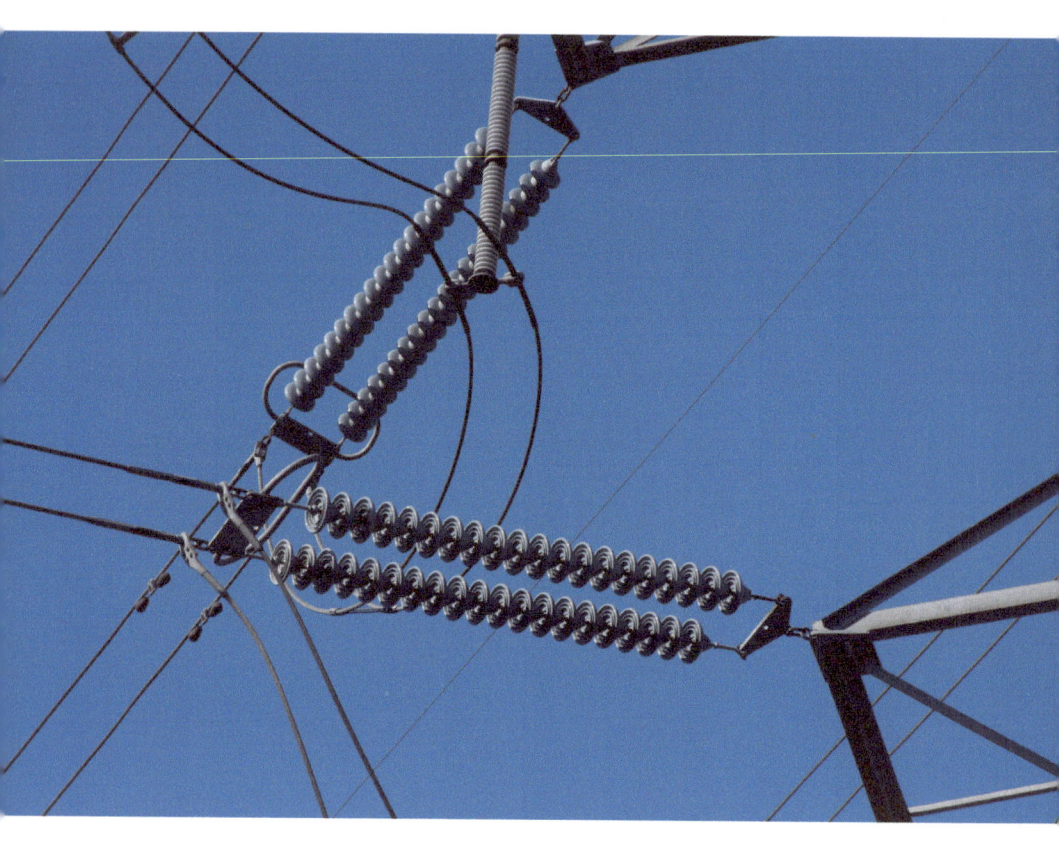

After dinner,
he dug another six feet.
He was down to 18 feet.
More hard work.
More sweat.
Very sore muscles.
But no water.

That's when he quit for the day.
The next day he dug another six feet.
The day after, another six.
The day after, another six.
He was down to 36 feet.

It had been hard work.
He was tired.
He had nothing to show for it.

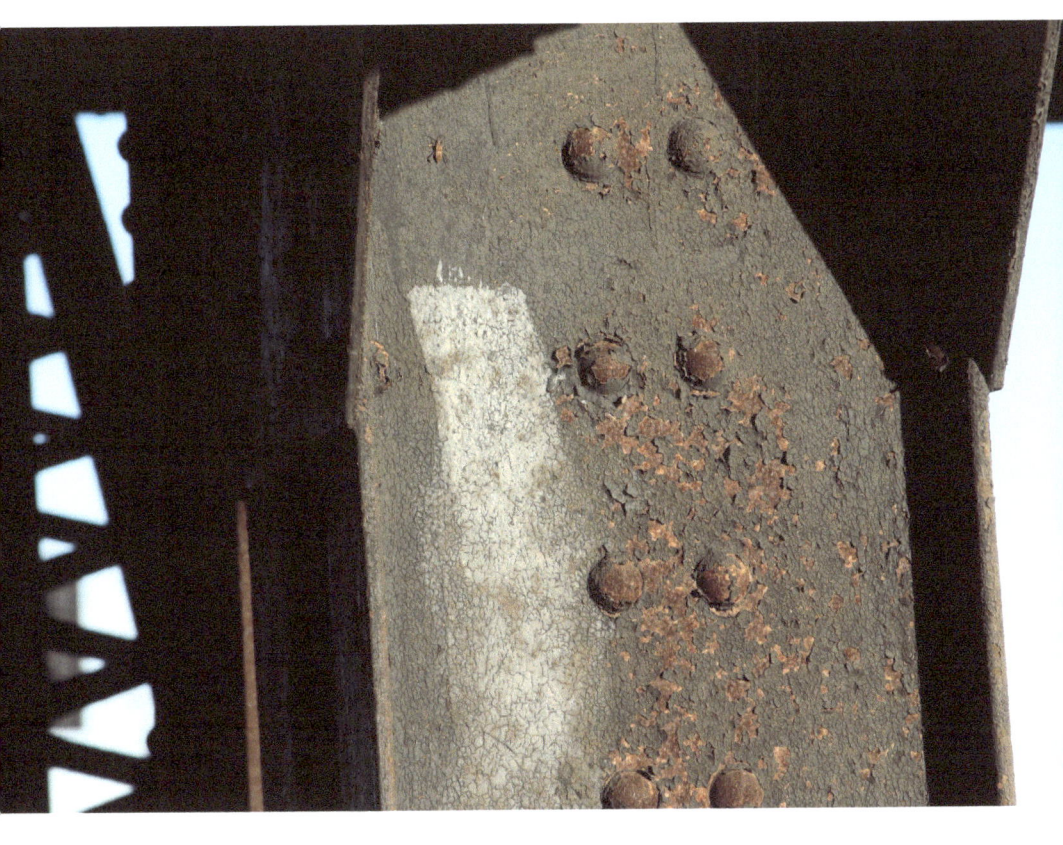

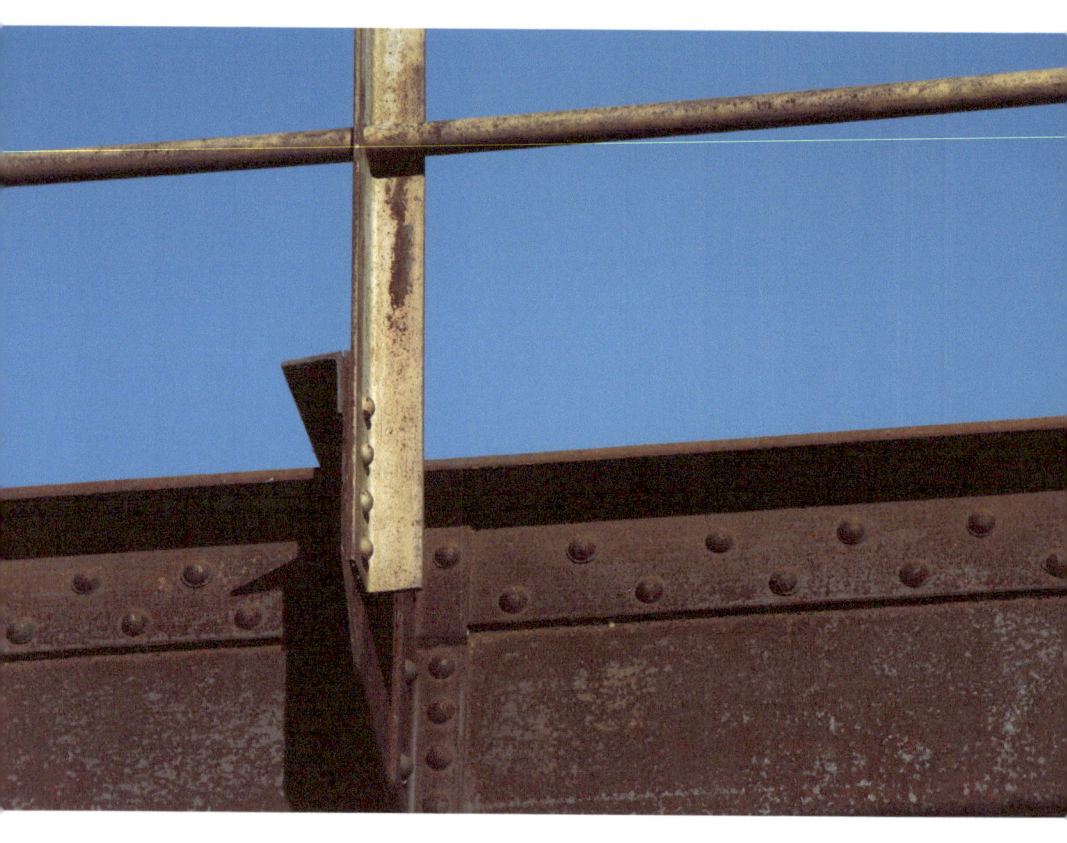

He was sore.
His back ached.
His arms ached.
His legs ached.

He hurt all over.
He went to bed.

The next day
he was too sore to work.
He got out a chair
and sat by the side of his well
and thought.

He needed water.
All this digging
was making him thirsty!

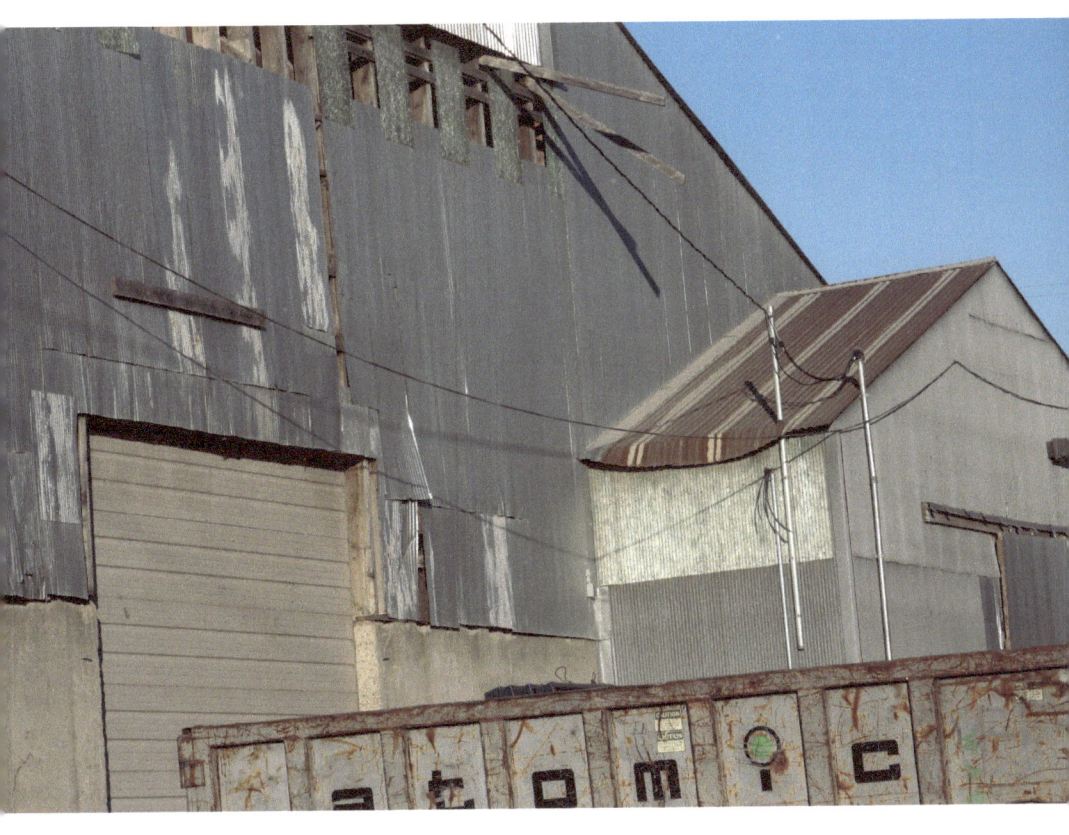

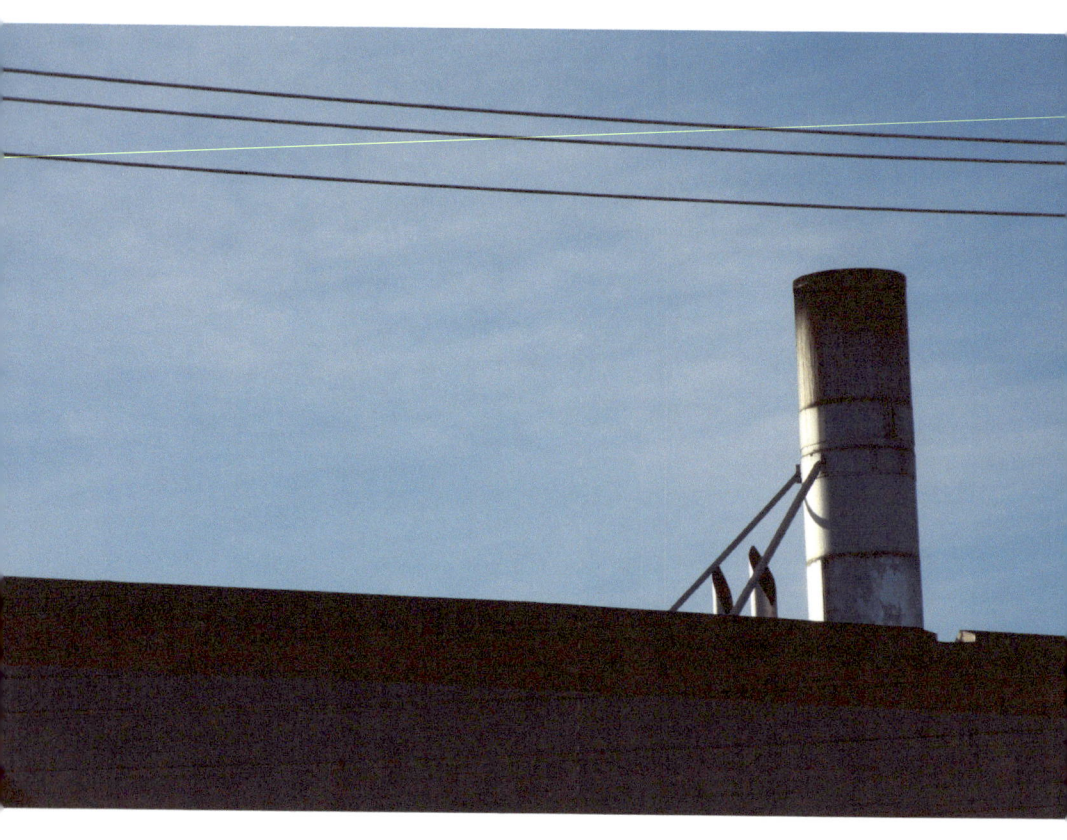

The digging was getting
harder and harder.
The topsoil had given way
to dirt mixed with stones.

The dirt mixed with stones
had given way
to stones mixed with dirt.

At 36 feet,
it was getting quite difficult
to haul the dirt out of the well,
it was so deep.

And on top of that,
it was a major construction job
to keep the sides of his well
from collapsing.

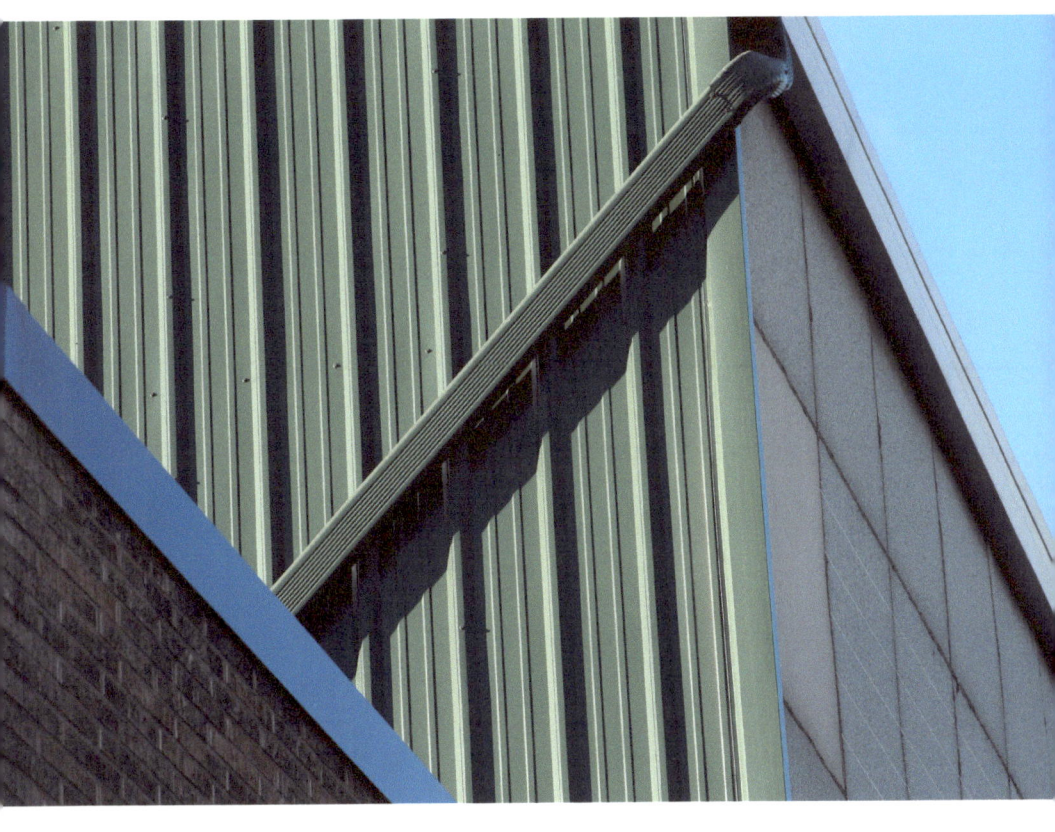

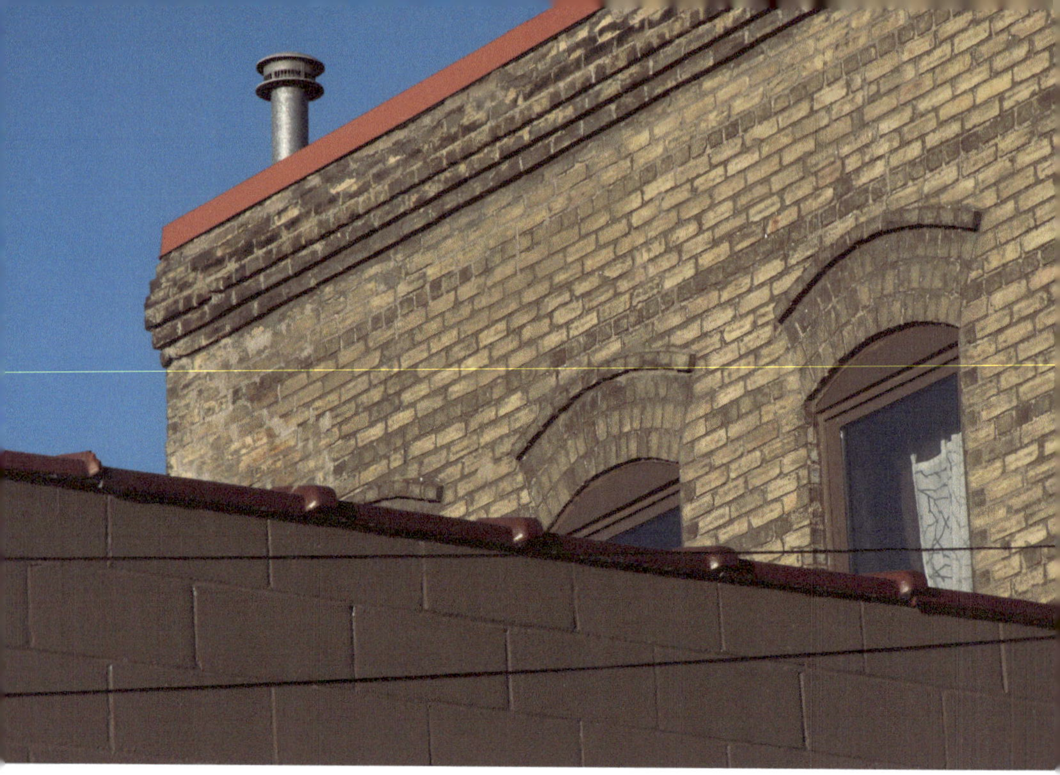

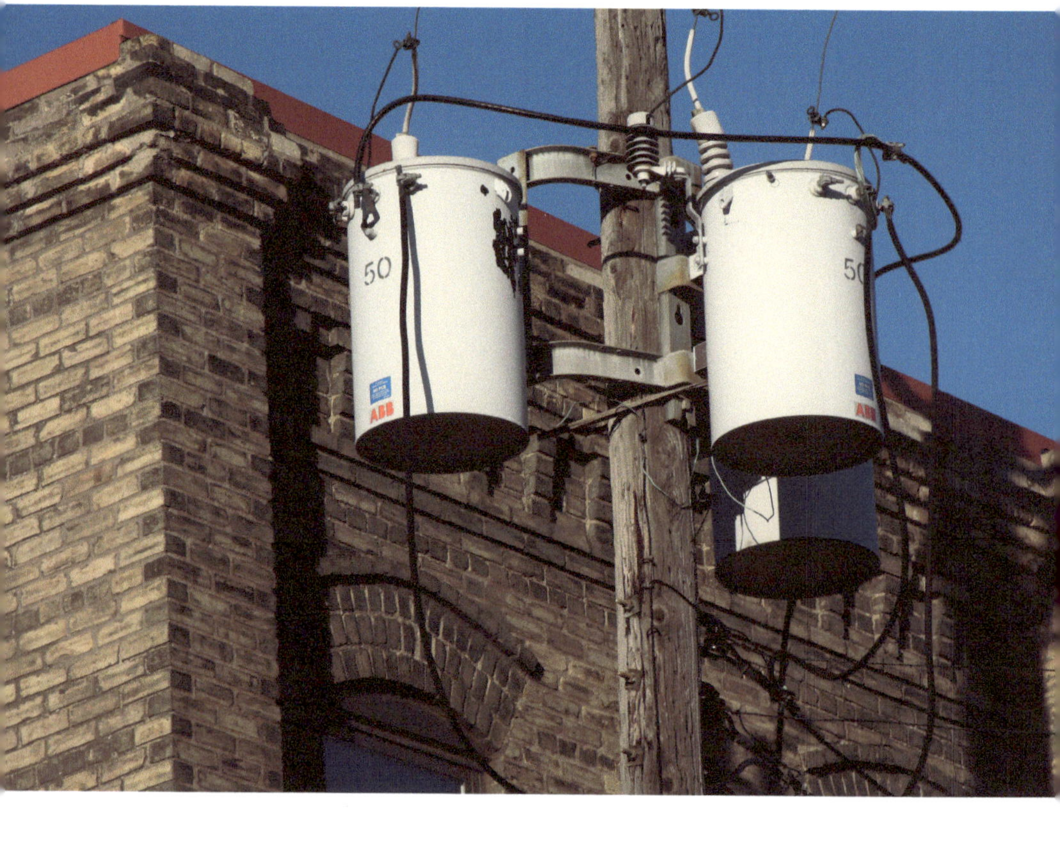
50
ABB

At least he could use the stones
to help create the sides of the well.

But it was hard, hard work.

It was going slower
and getting more painful.
He was worn out each day.
And he was getting nowhere.

After taking a day off,
he decided to keep going.

Maybe he was persistent.
Maybe he was just stubborn.
Maybe he just didn't know what else to do.

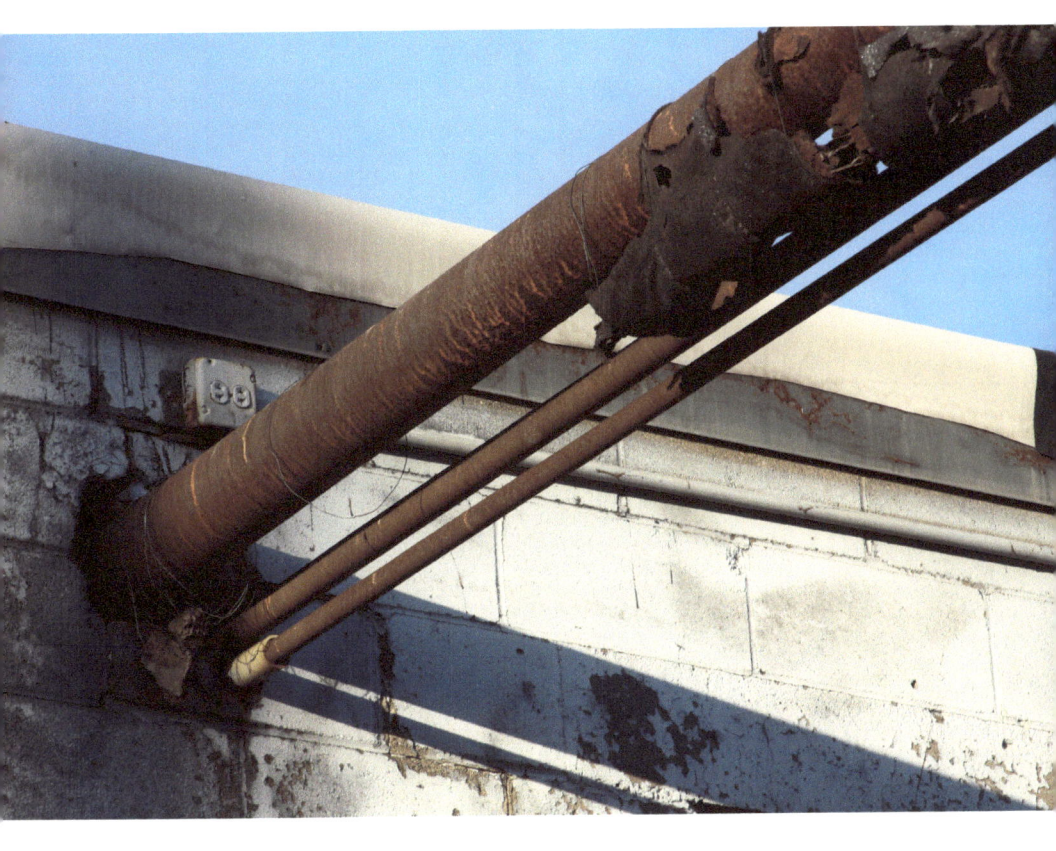

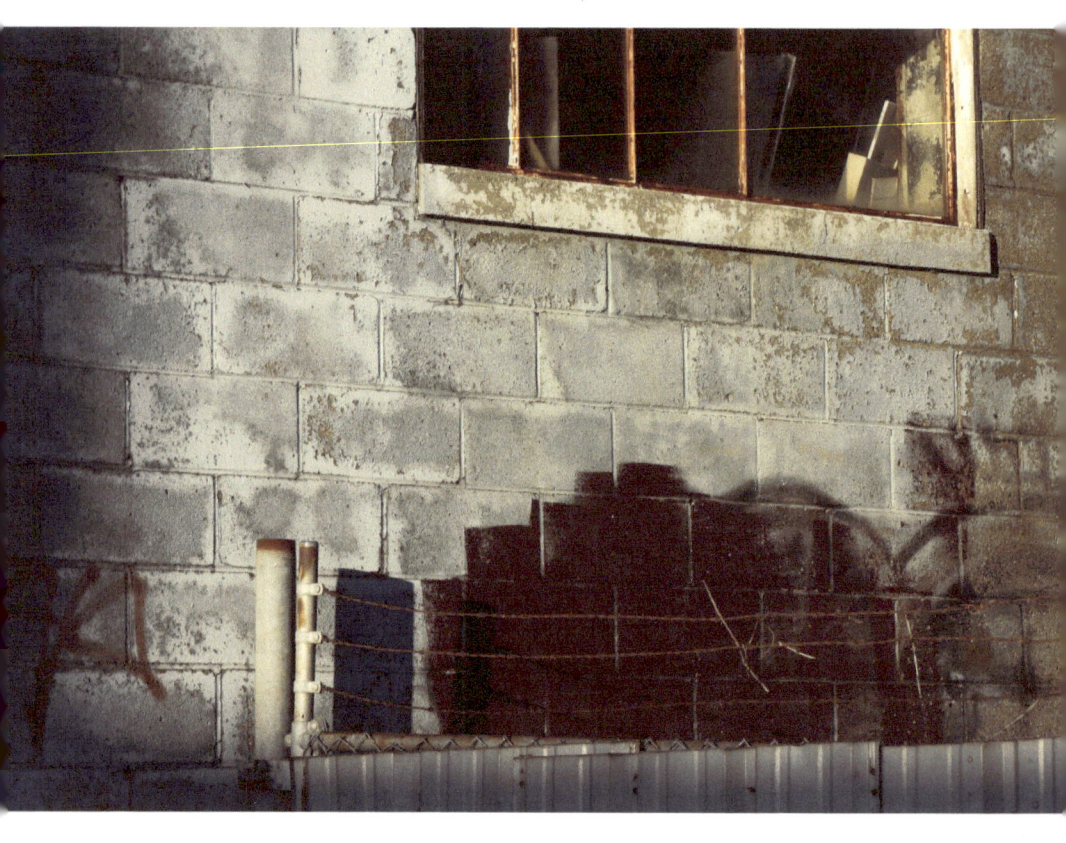

After a few more days
he was down to 48 feet.
Still no water.

He kept going.

People were starting
to make fun of Roger
and his well.

"A shaft to nowhere" some called it.
Others called it the Dirt Well.

"Put your bucket
down the Dirt Well," they said.
"Roger,
way down in the bottom of the well,
will fill your bucket
with rocks and dirt for you.
You can't get any water
from Roger's well,
but you can get free dirt."

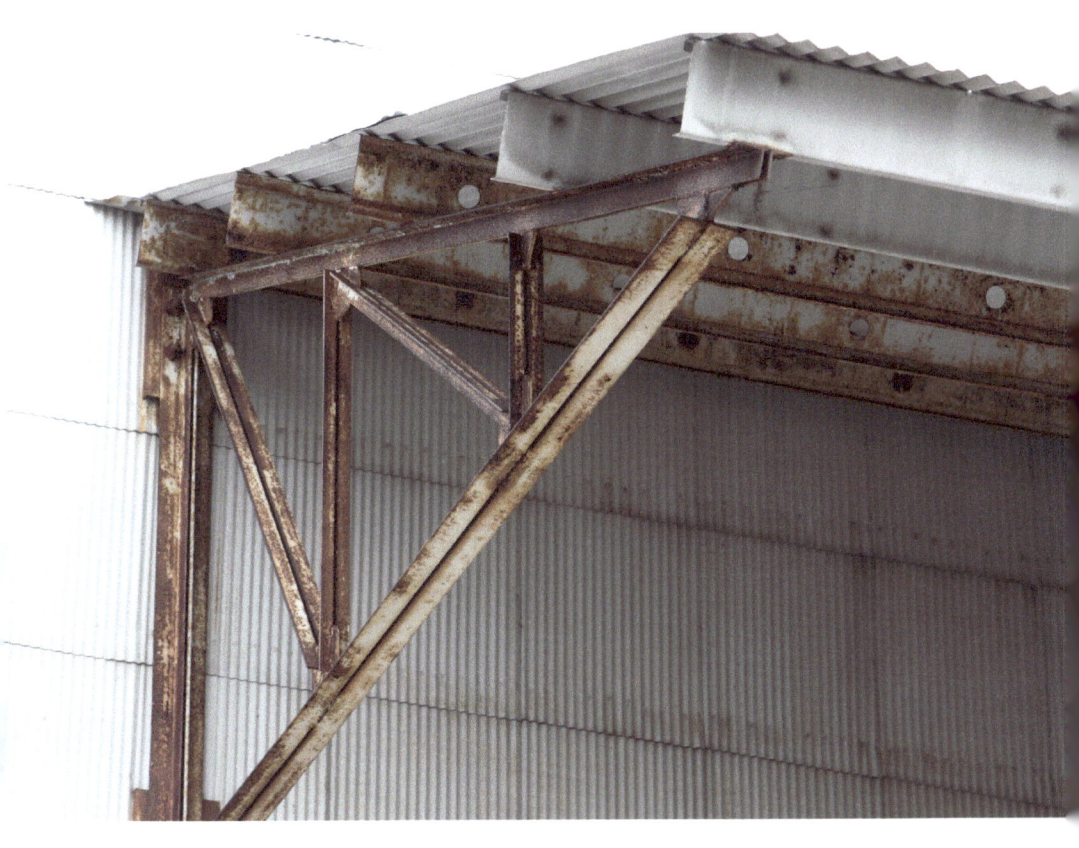

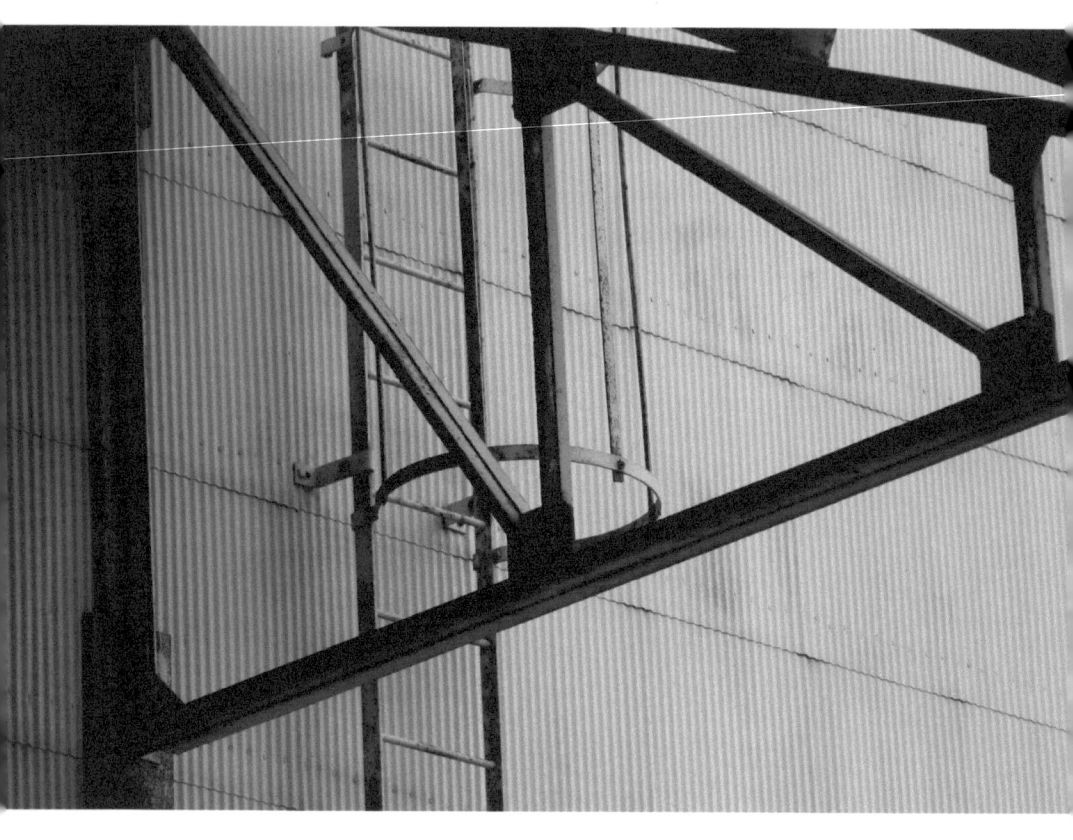

The neighborhood kids
made up a sing-song rhyme
about Roger's well.

He heard it one night
as he crawled out of his well,
too exhausted to sleep.

Roger thought about their laughter
and their songs and their comments
when he worked the next few days.

He kept digging,
even though he was discouraged.

Sometimes Roger found it hard
to stay focused.
But when he ran out of steam,
his thirst reminding him
why he was digging.

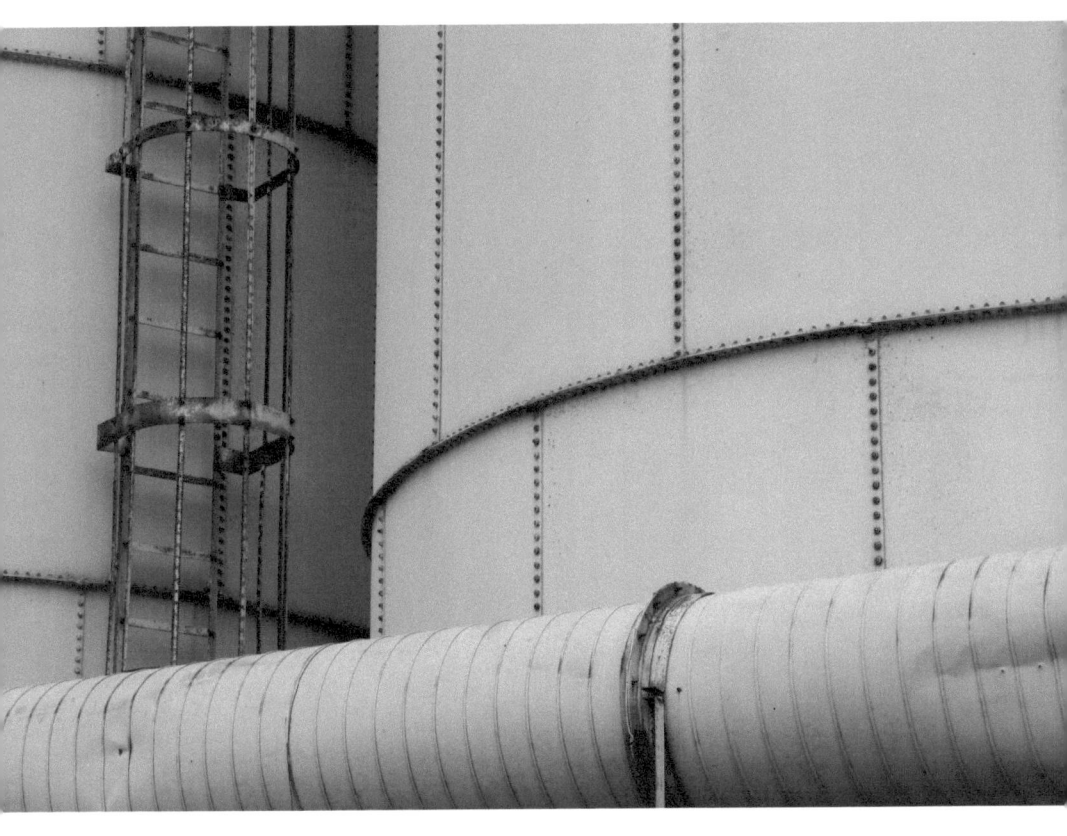

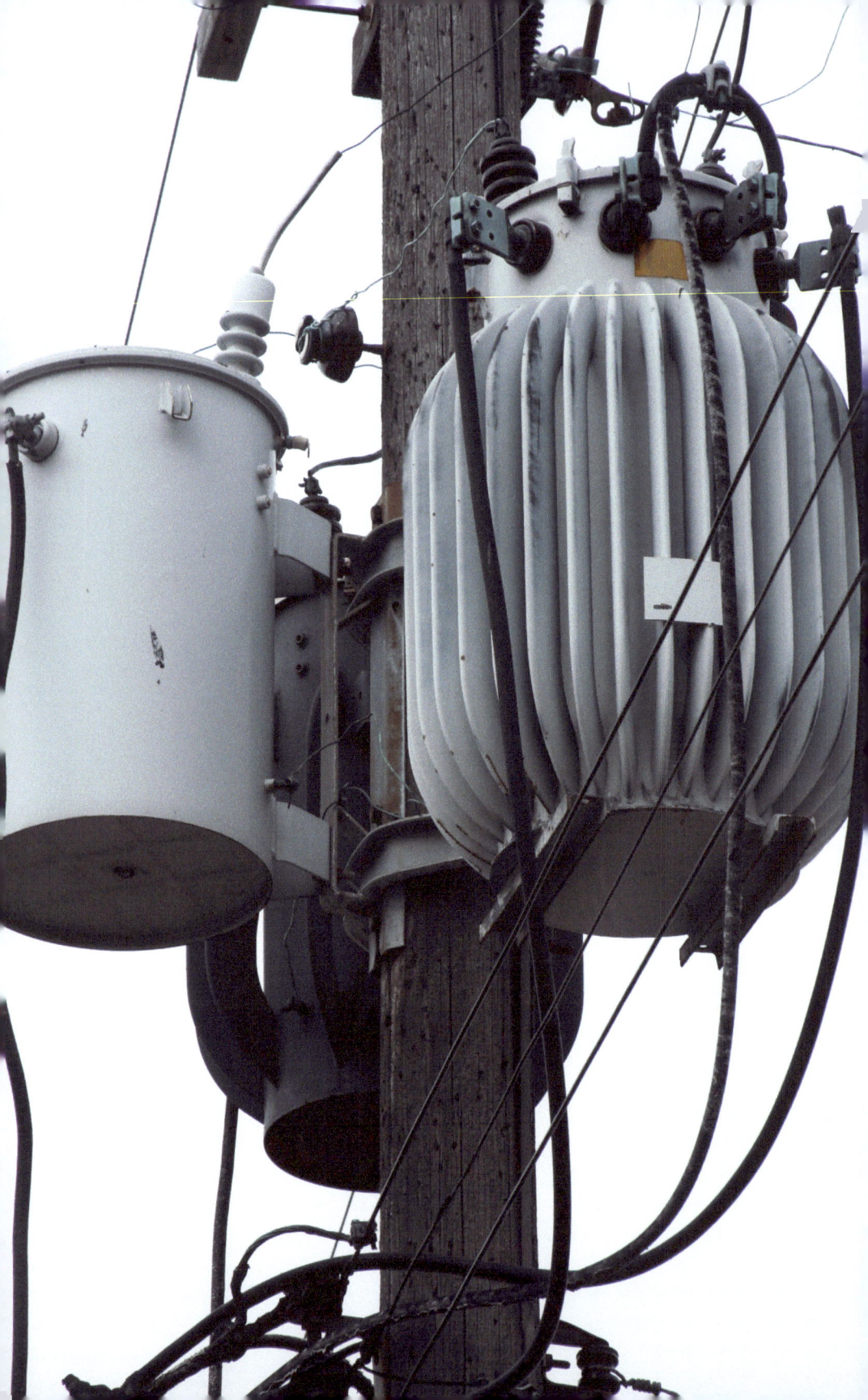

Some days he only dug
another couple of feet.
Faster progress was impossible
because it was so hard
to get the supplies
for the sides of the well
all the way down
to where he needed them.

And it was a long way
to haul dirt out of the well.

You might think
this is the time in the story
for Roger to get a good break.

But then it got even harder.

The stones in his way
became bigger.
Some were too heavy to lift
and had to be split apart.

He kept digging anyway.
Slower.
51 feet.
53 feet.
55 feet.
56 feet.
57 feet.

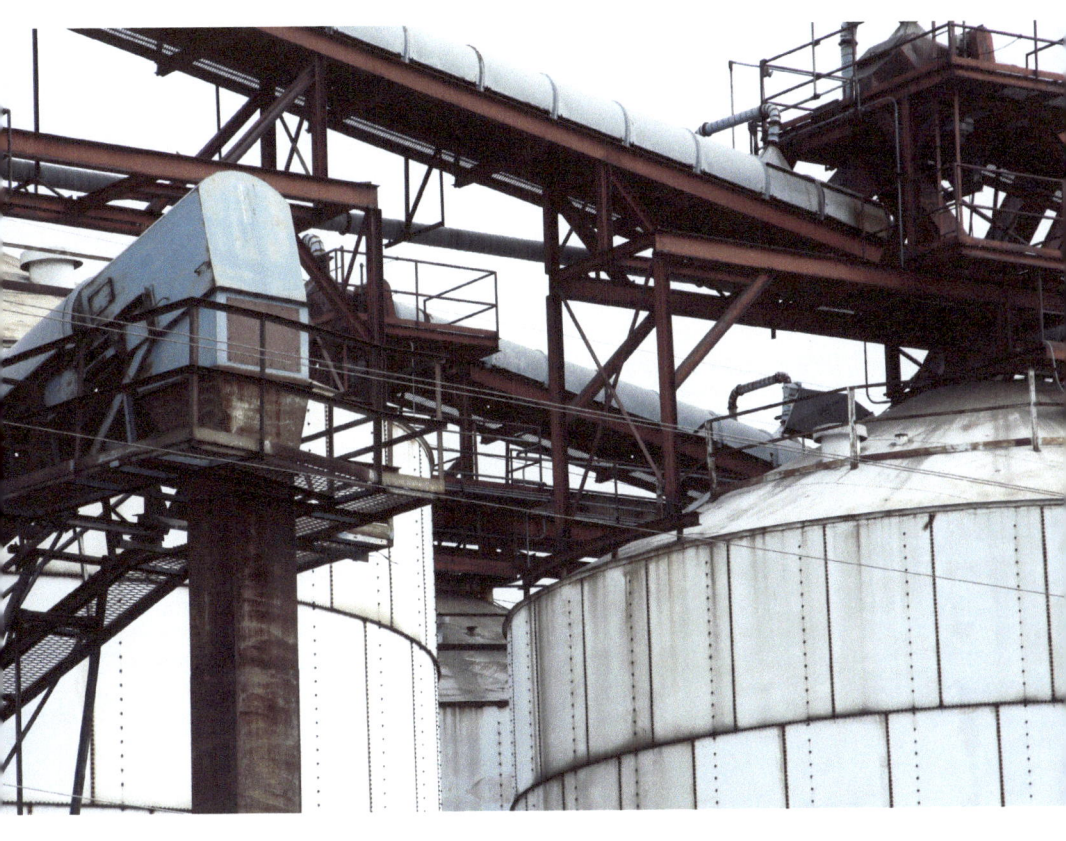

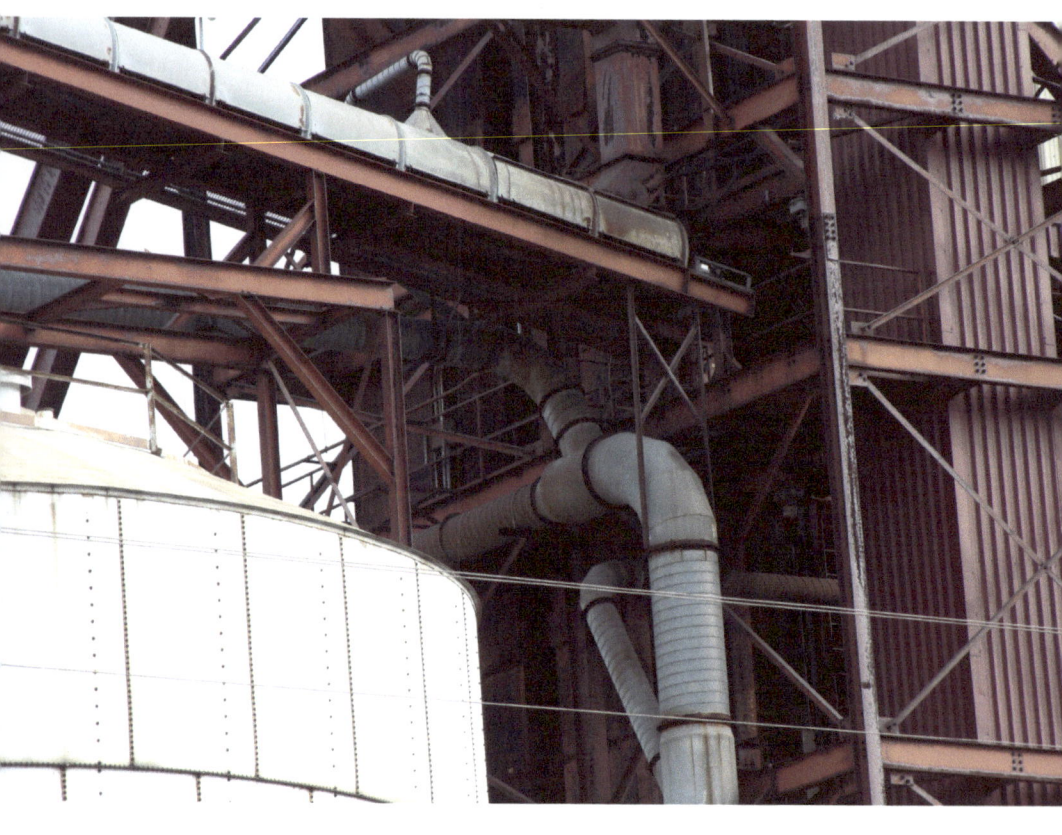

Roger was approaching exhaustion.

There was not a lot of air,
57 feet down.
And there was no water
to show for all his work.
I *did* mention that Roger was hoping for water?

His back ached.
His muscles ached.
He thought about quitting
all the time he was working.
At night he dreamed of quitting.
He even started
singing the songs of quitting
that the neighborhood kids
had made up.

Maybe his neighbors were right.

All his effort so far had been useless.
There was no water
to show for all his trouble.

Then at 58 feet,
he hit bedrock.
Not dirt and stones.
Not stones and dirt.
Not giant rocks.
Just a solid mantle of stone.
Something you could only chip at
with a pick-axe
– and not very quickly,
at that.

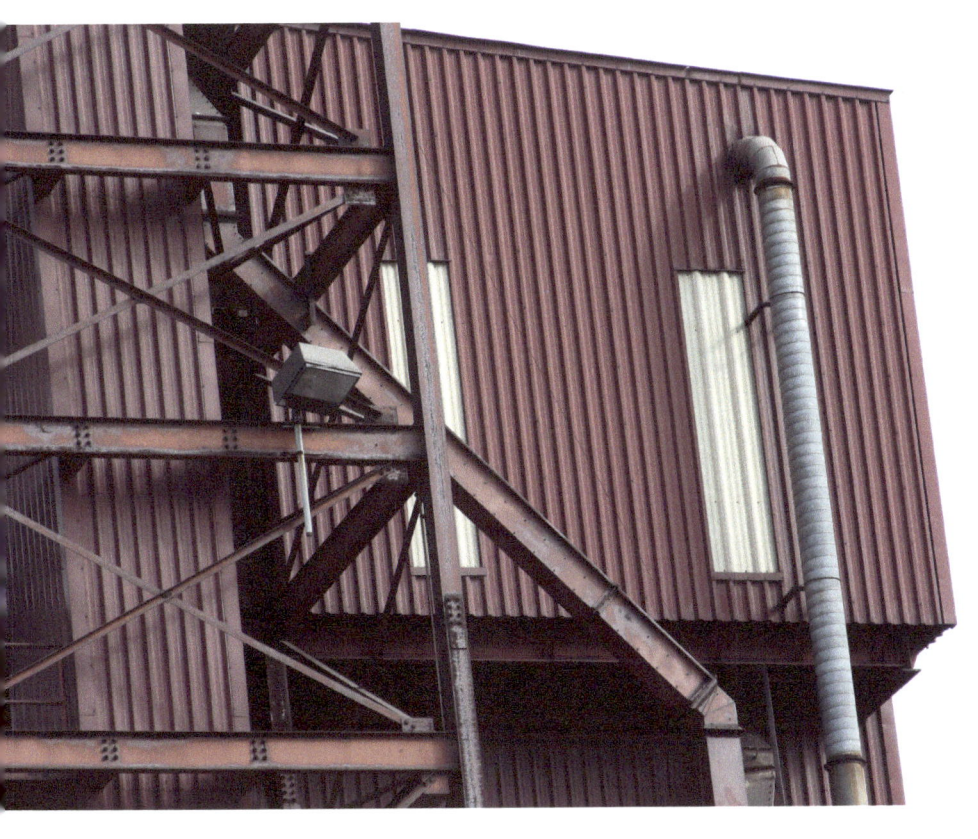

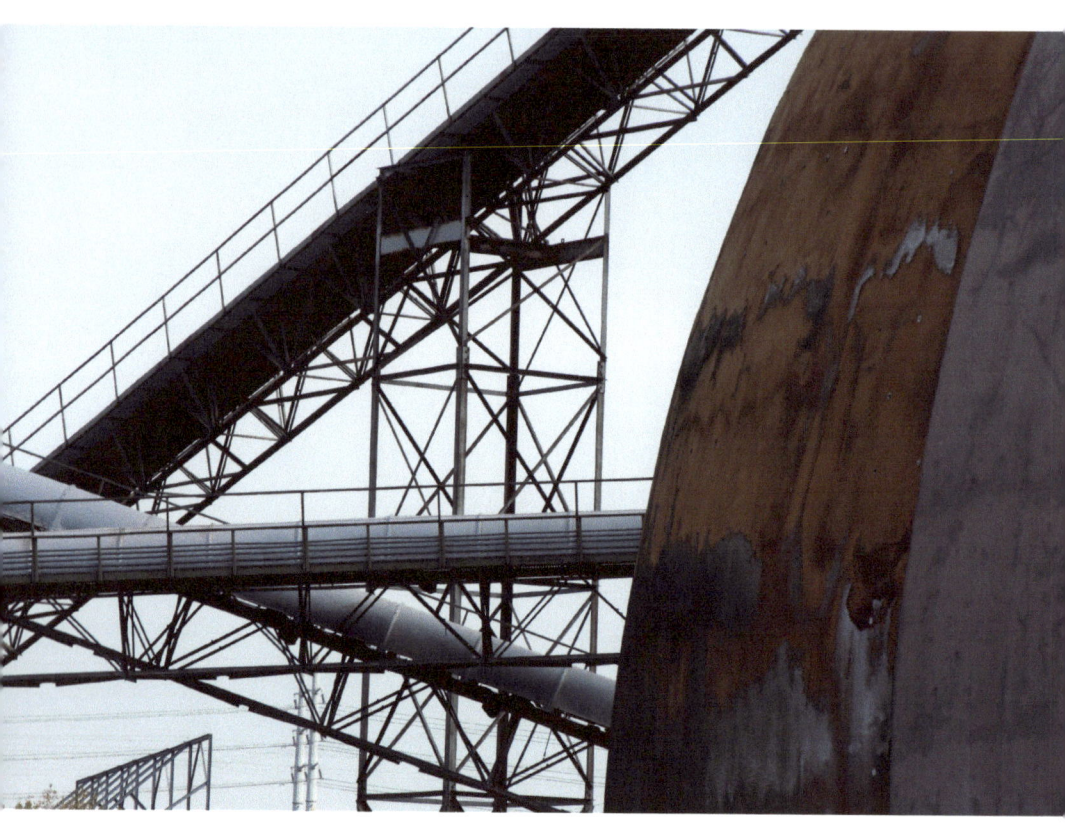

He wasn't progressing
by feet any more.

Now his well was getting deeper
by quarter-inches.

Roger was exhausted,
tired,
and sad.

All that effort.
No water.
And now, bedrock.

For three more days
Roger struggled to chip away the rock
at the bottom of his well.

The bedrock he'd hit
was nearly impassible.

By the end of the next three days,
he'd only made it
to 60 feet.

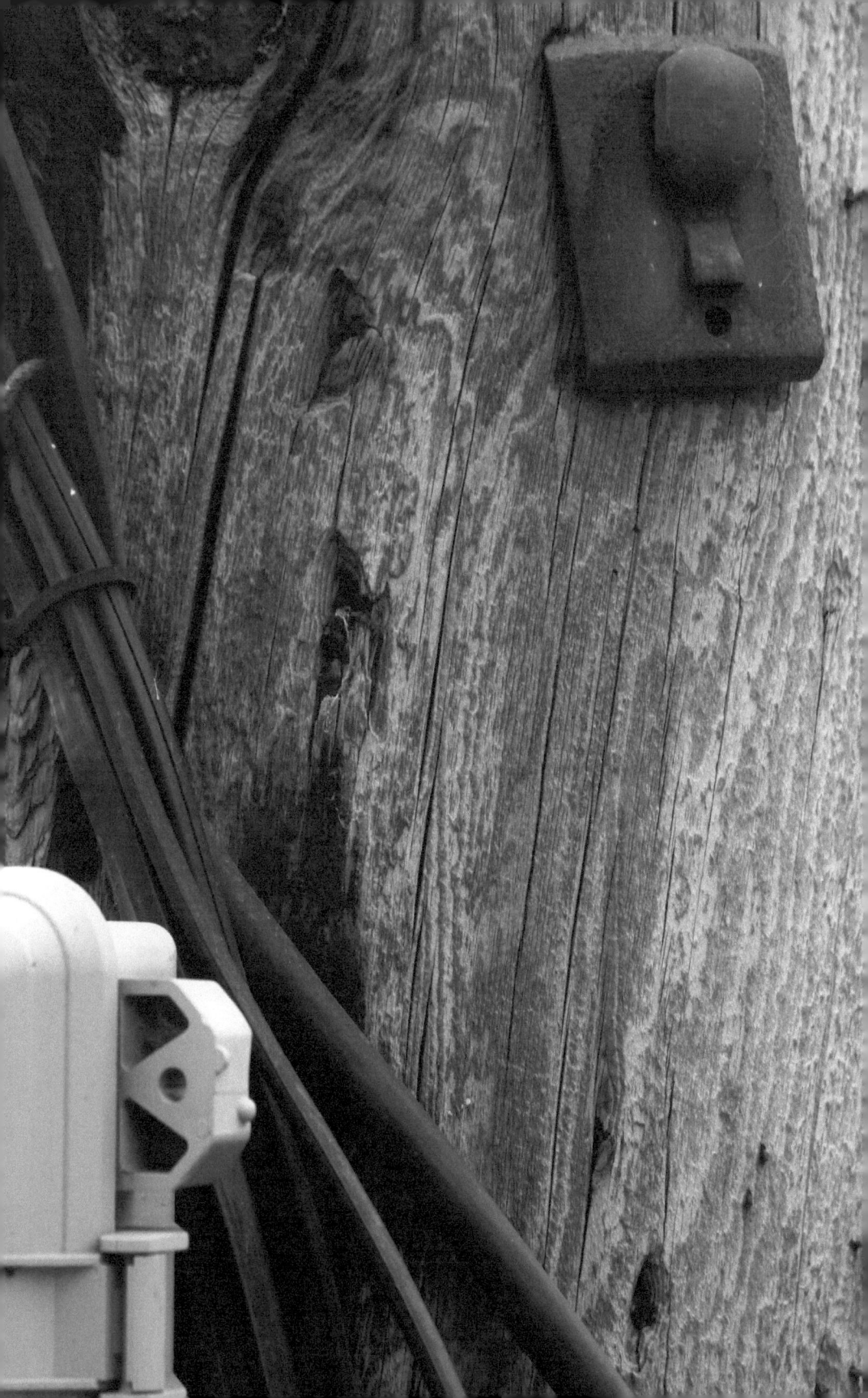

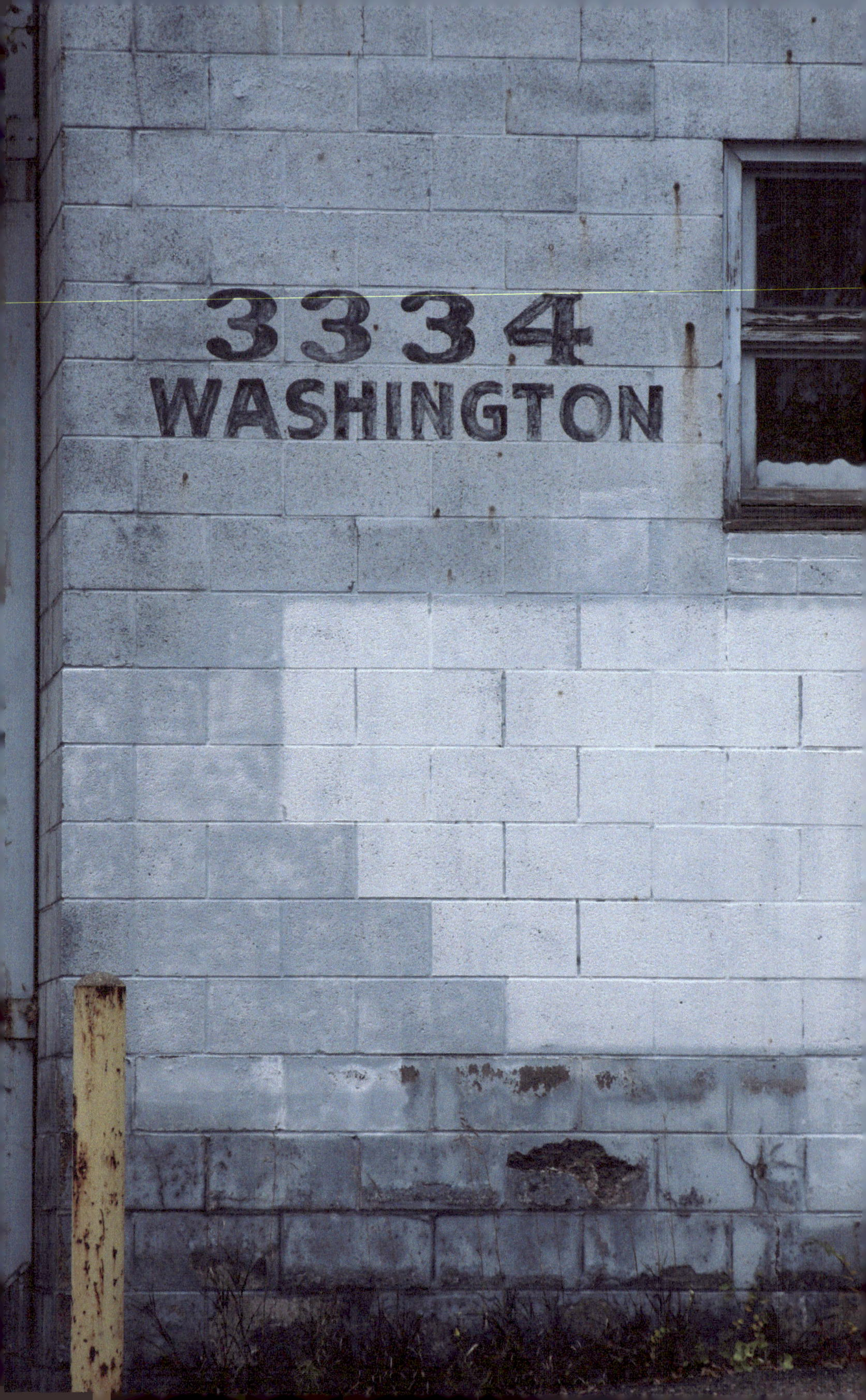
3334
WASHINGTON

There was no sign of water.
Just more rock.

Roger finally got some sense.
He finally listened to his neighbors.

He hauled his pickaxe to the surface.
He hoisted himself out of the well one last time.
He lay by the side of the well,
exhausted,
spent.
And he quit.

He'd dug 60 feet straight down.
He'd created a beautiful well,
with well-constructed sides.
His well had a turn-crank at the top of it
and a bucket with a long rope
and a roof over it.
But the bucket just went down to bedrock.
Not water.

All that effort,
and Roger hadn't accomplished a thing.

~ ~ ~

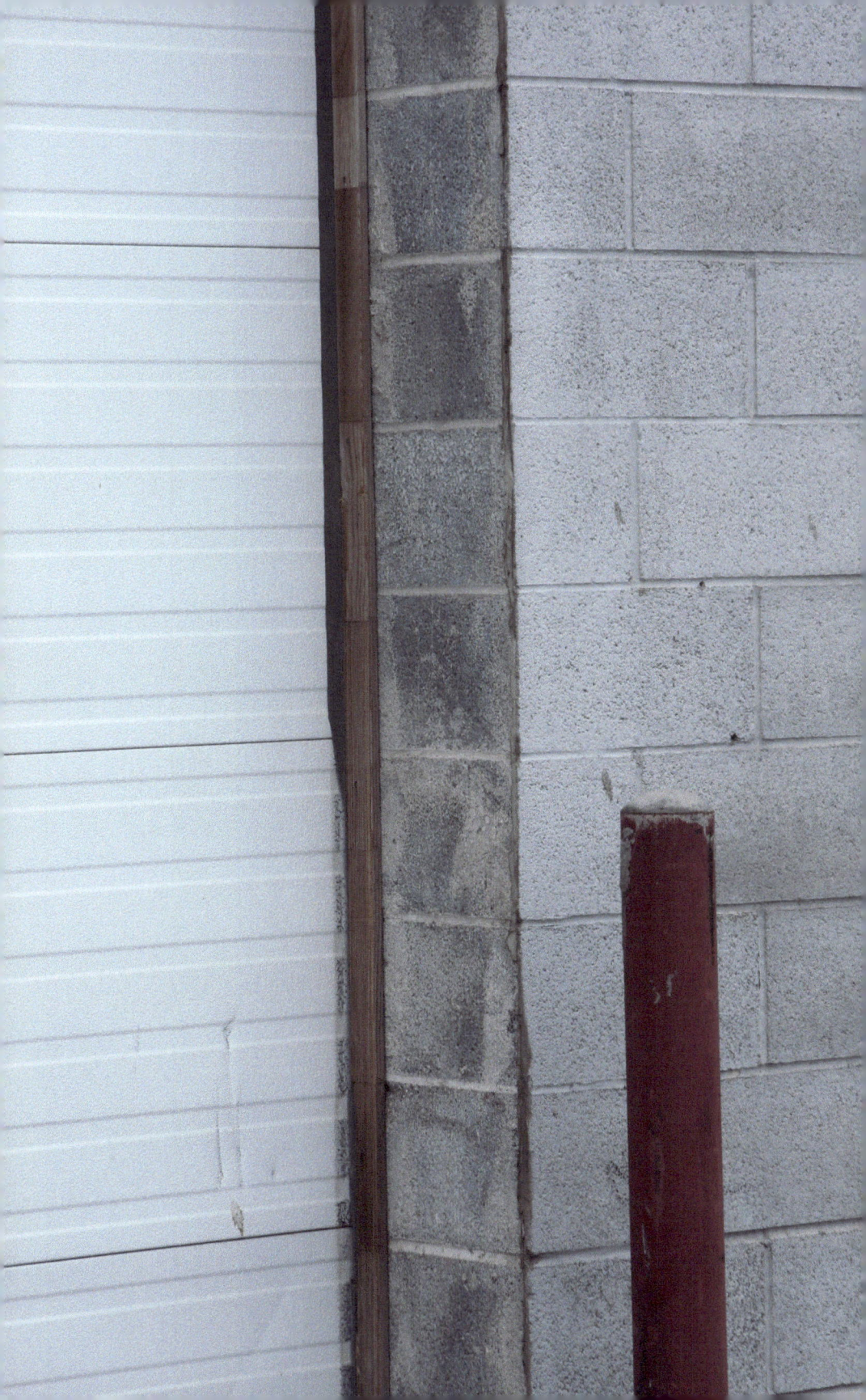

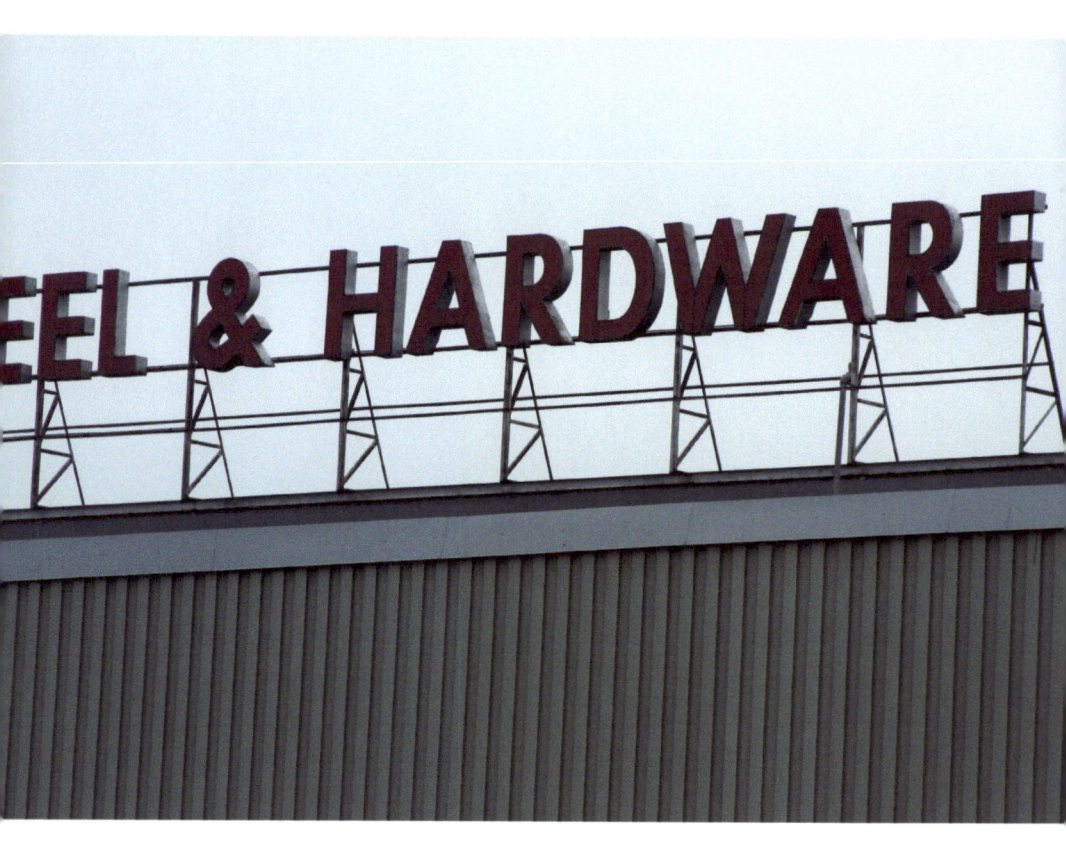

Reflection Questions

Do you agree that
Roger didn't accomplish anything?

If someone else comes along
and digs the remaining foot
and gets to water,
should they get credit for it?

How much?

How can people tell
if they should quit or keep going?

Would it change your answers if you knew
there was no water at all
where Roger was digging?

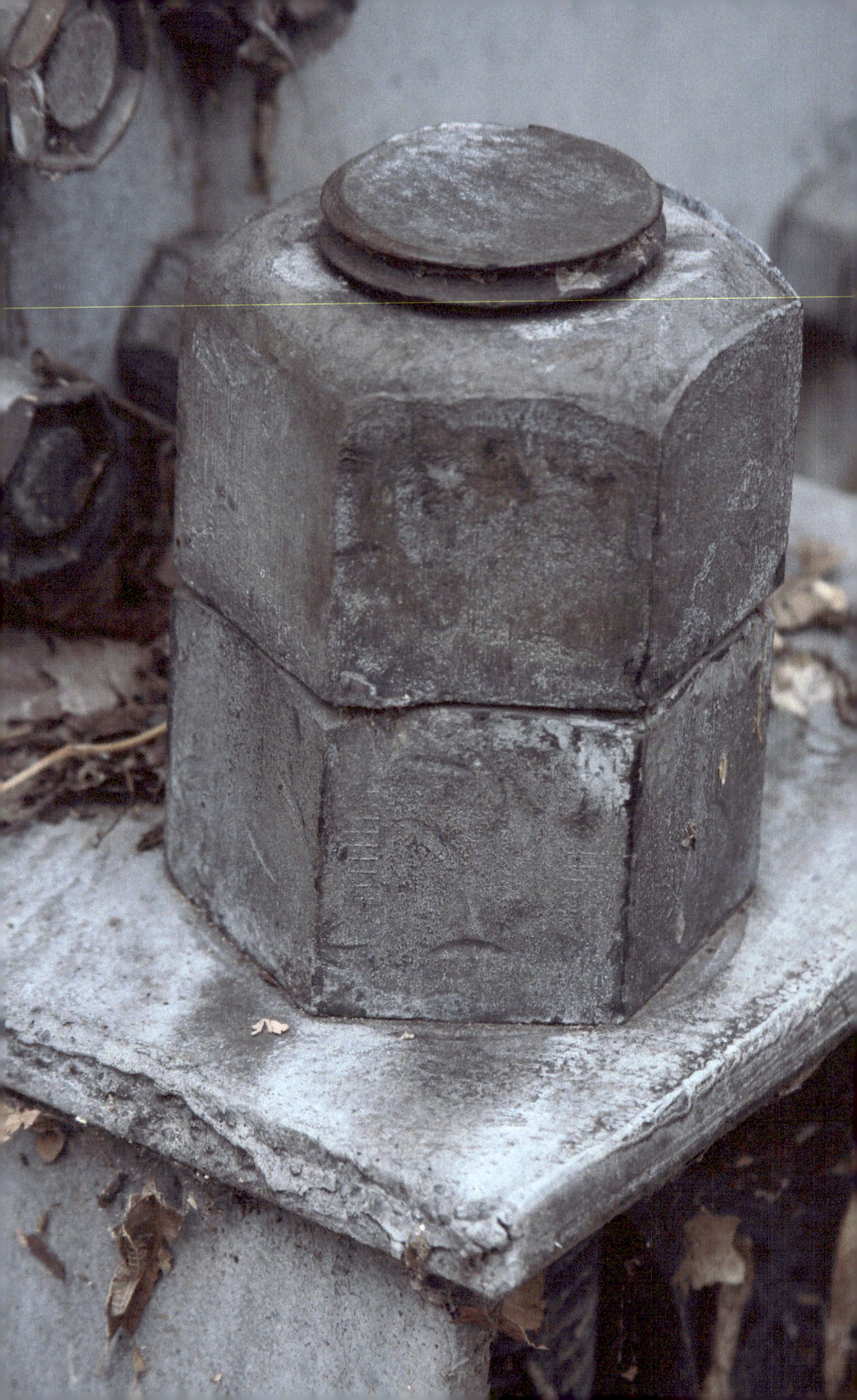

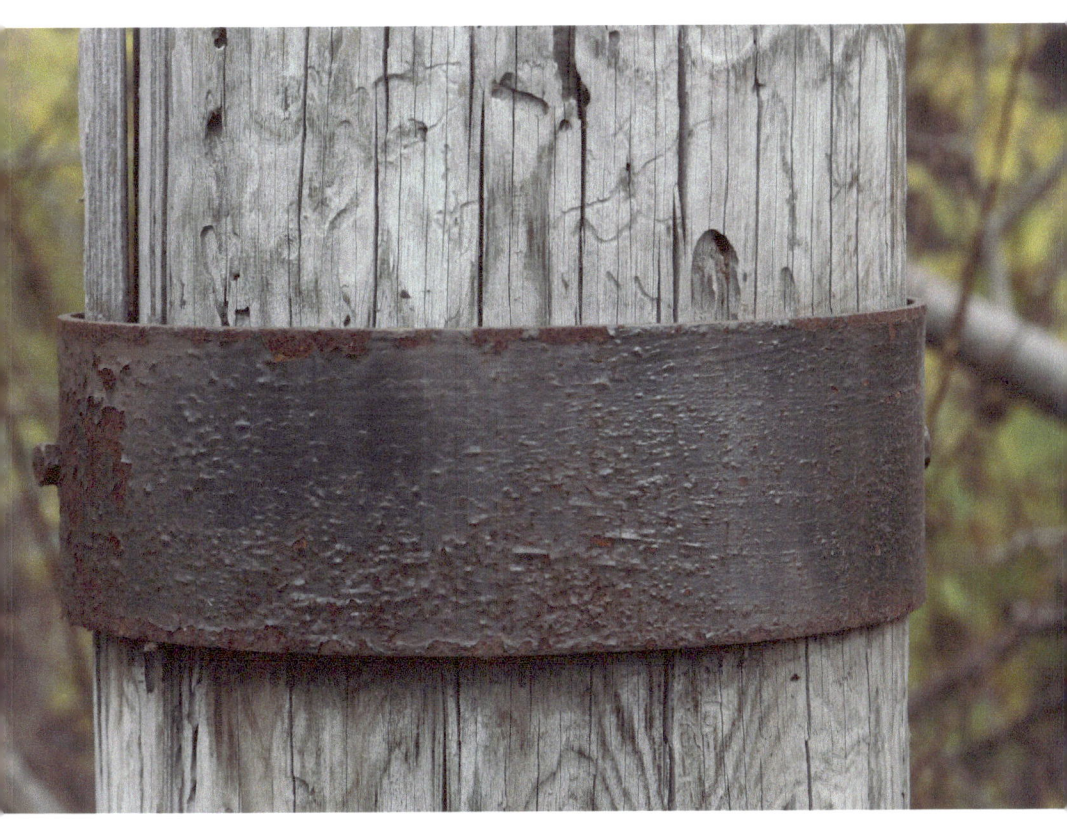

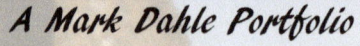
A Mark Dahle Portfolio

Farmer Jane

This Mark Dahle Portfolio includes a beautiful painting, twenty-five gorgeous photographs from the Netherlands, and the story of Farmer Jane.

Jane didn't know that farmers have troubles.

But she was about to discover how *many* troubles they have.

An Assignment From Hell

This Mark Dahle Portfolio includes a gorgeous painting, twenty-six beautiful photographs of electric distribution, and a story about America's wealth.

When you're in hell, you don't want to be called into the boss's office.

No matter how it goes, you always know that no good will come of it.

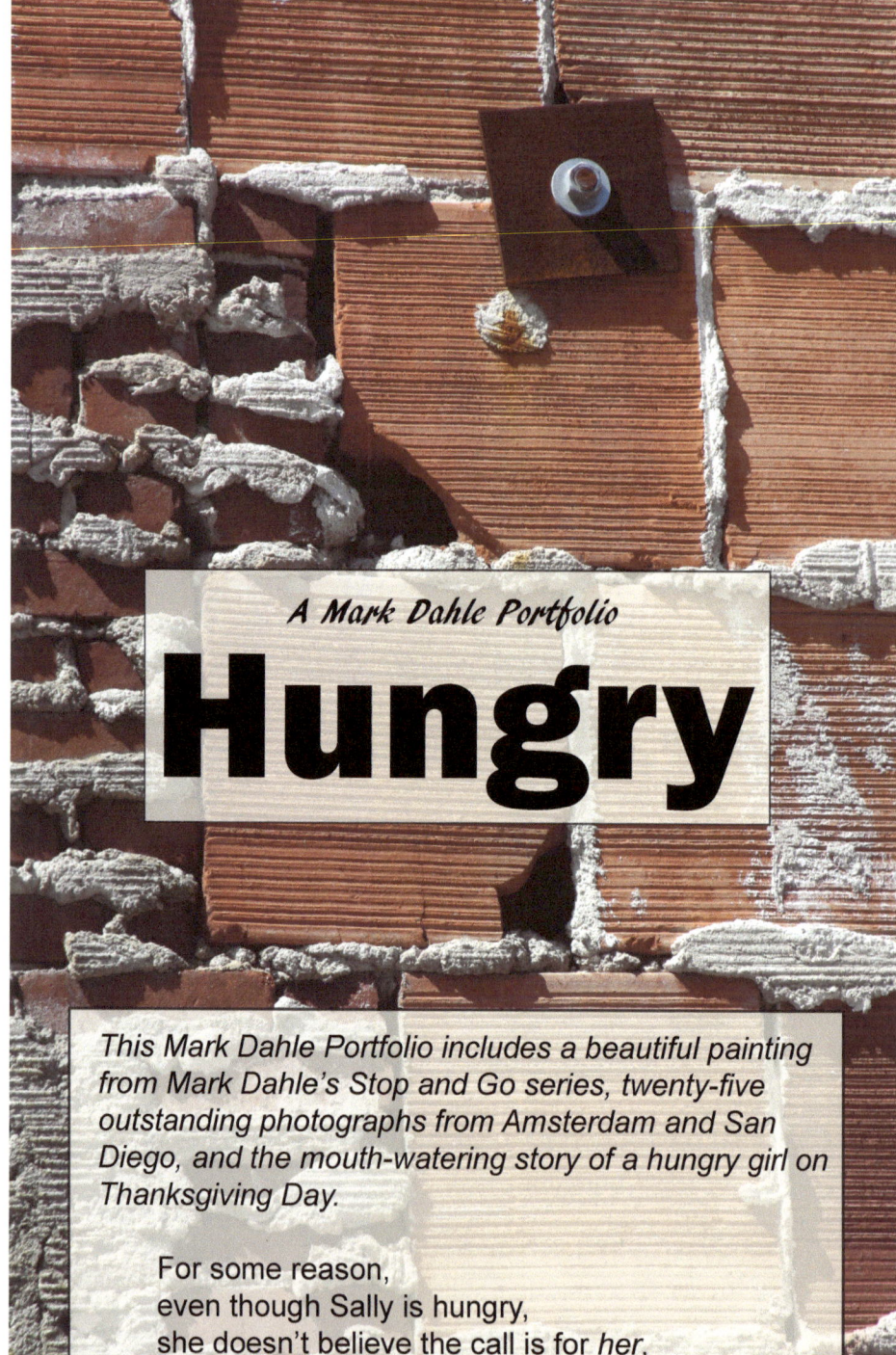

A Mark Dahle Portfolio

Hungry

This Mark Dahle Portfolio includes a beautiful painting from Mark Dahle's Stop and Go series, twenty-five outstanding photographs from Amsterdam and San Diego, and the mouth-watering story of a hungry girl on Thanksgiving Day.

For some reason,
even though Sally is hungry,
she doesn't believe the call is for *her*,
at least not right now.